SIDES

SECOND EDITION

Phoenix illustrated by Pournima Shahapure
and modified by Radhika Pande

SIDES

SECOND EDITION

APEKSHA KADAM

I've felt
my own fire,
burned myself down
for you
a thousand times

But, now, I'll write
in this darkness
about all those nights
and rise like a phoenix
with blue eyes

To my lovely best friend,
to the best younger brother in this world
and to me

I love you all

Contents

Acknowledgement

I want to say a big big Thank You to Pournima di for encouraging me to write this book. It wouldn't have existed without you.

I'm deeply grateful to Pournima di and Radhika for the beautiful cover and to my little brother, Aditya, for trying his best not to disturb me when I was writing. I love you!

And to me. For everything I did for me.

Dear Reader,

Have you ever been through something so deeply disturbing that you still struggle to speak about it? And was it someone close, maybe a friend, who offered you that pain and refused to offer you an apology after it? Because I have. And I would like to share it with you as much as I can.

Which is why I should tell you this before the poetry begins: that I tried my best to form the words. But my mere thoughts and my attempts at constructing those words have always risked something huge collapsing inside me. And if I am being honest with you, my dear reader, today, I don't know how to be brave enough to talk about it. But let me also tell you this: that this story has a lot more than that. I can promise you that.

So, dear reader, would you like to take a chance on me? Because in the future, I think. I might be able to tell you the entire story.

Apeksha,
the poet

No End

Your side in me screams
'Stop shaming me'

And my side in me says
'I'm listening, tell me'

A coin has two sides
so I tried to understand yours before mine
But that night walk,
the other night's talk
and the last night
woke me up and
made me realise

that my side should've always, always,
been tainted by mine
and that your side should've never, never, been
above my side

And yes, I know tonight, I know
that my side of this story
is tainted by my side
so maybe, maybe,
I'm not painting the picture right
for everyone to see
or maybe, maybe, I am
because this is how it should've been
all of this time
my side tainted by mine

Part of my mind keeps judging me
and part of my mind keeps defending me

I feel so terrible to tell this tale
and I feel such a relief to be able to share it this way

My mind is screaming at me
in a hundred different ways
and my mind is proving my case
in a hundred different ways

All of this spiralling because
because your side in me cannot stop blaming me
as I write in detail what your words did to me
while my side in me is helping me process
as I write in detail what your words said to me

All of this stormy rain
and barely glimpses of a clear sky
just because your side in me
refuses to understand
that it's not just about what you said that night
that it's more about what I faced after that night

I feel anger, resentment, understanding, and spite
every emotion at the same time
then I feel guilty for sharing this with the world
even though I know it's going to make me fine

Sometimes, I really, really, wish I could hate you
and leave it at that
But I can't, I just can't
because even if the pain drowns me in my own mind
it doesn't mask my eyes
it doesn't make me blind
so now I can see
there were times you were good to me
there were times you were good for me

But then, suddenly,
my mind comes back to that night
and I feel anger, resentment, understanding, and spite
every emotion at the same time

So, then, I think of forgiveness
thinking now I would be free and fine
only to drown all over again in my own mind
because sometimes,
sometimes, forgiveness seems too kind

Tonight, I thought of writing to you
writing-
I'm sorry I felt insecure, I'm sorry I felt tamed
I'm sorry, I let you go first and
I'm sorry our friendship couldn't sustain

I was going to say-
I'm heartbroken to lose a friend
and I am well aware
you have lost one too, on your end

And sometimes, I wish,
I could comfort you through it
against my better judgement
But then I think
Would you do the same
because I too am dealing?

But now, as I'm writing and writing
I am recalling the past too
and now I can see clearly
that you knew I was walking away
and you let me go too
that you saw me walking away
and you didn't stop me too

That Night

The memory of
how casually you said it
is still burning in my mind
The memory of
how casual you were after you said it
is still torturing my mind

My addiction to night walks is why
I continued walking with our common friends
and you that night
even though I didn't want to be
anywhere you were that night

I keep wondering to myself
is my addiction to night walks the reason why
I had to suffer days and nights in my own mind
after that night
I keep wondering to myself
if only I had learnt sooner
the art of enjoying my own company
during night walks
I wouldn't have put myself
in harm's way that night

That night, something in me told me-
Refuse to walk or regret your choice
and I couldn't choose
so I asked my feet for advice

And now, here I am
cannot stop thinking about how I would have been
if only, if only, I would have refused to walk that night

I zoned myself out
for most part of the walk
and I could barely hear about
what the talk was
because if years of being friends with you
has taught me something, it's this-
that you could never help yourself
from making fun of people
in a crowd of more than two
and you did that because it amused you

So, like every single time
I zoned myself out of this conversation too
so I don't have to put myself in that position
like I had done several times before,
before, I had to learn not to

And till this day, I wish, I wish,
I had stayed that way
lost in the trees on my left
and in my own thoughts astray
Because then I wouldn't have heard what I heard,
I wouldn't have felt what I felt,
I wouldn't have faced what I faced
and I would've,
I would've been fine in my own mind

Lost in my own thoughts
I was lecturing myself,
reminding myself over and over again
to never say yes if I am not sure
to never put myself in a place
I don't want to be in, I'm sure
to be better for myself
because I deserve so

But then, suddenly, I zoned in
without my knowledge
and I swear, I swear,
I tried so hard to get lost again
in the trees on my left I was looking at
But I couldn't
I just couldn't
so I let myself be
thinking at least half the road is behind me
thinking I just need to survive the other half
to get it over with

How wrong I was!
Oh, how wrong I was!
For I still go back
to that other half of the road
and back to that night walk

We all turned round a u-turn to head back home
I heard you talking, and this time, I just couldn't ignore

You were talking non-stop
and that's when you said what you said that night
without giving it a second thought in your own mind

What you said
was so unacceptably terribly bad tonight
that I couldn't even make myself to share it
with my best friends
for more than a month after that night
even as we were spending hours and hours together
that month after that night
Because I kept thinking to myself
they don't deserve to know what you said that night
they don't deserve to know what you said that night

And I wish, I so wish,
I could write it down and share this
with the world
so I can at least, at least, be fine
but then it risks someone else's mind
someone, anyone who has been through
what I have been through in my life
And I know it, I know it,
because every time I remember your words from that night
my head hurts every single time

I couldn't believe my ears
and what your words indicated
But I still waited, waited thinking
thinking that any second now
I'm going to hear an apology
because I presumed
you might have heard your own words by now

But all I heard was silence
and that you were silent for too long

So, expecting an apology, I looked at you,
and I was so shocked,
when I realised that you hadn't even noticed
the seriousness of your own words
as you said them out loud tonight
as you said them out loud tonight

And all I wanted to do was scream at you,
show every ounce of anger I felt towards you
But I had to gather myself together
to get my words right in front of you
Because I knew, I knew,
when someone points out to you
you're flawed
you always, always, get defensive
even when you are nowhere near right
at all

I pulled myself together
even as I was falling apart
and I spoke with clear words
and clearly anger-toned voice
when I said,
'It's inappropriate and inhuman
what you just said
and never ever repeat it
in front of anybody else
Do you understand me?'

And for a few seconds
that everyone was quiet
I still heard no apology coming from you
But then you joined in the conversation
within a second
when a new topic was introduced

And then, I heard you
talking and laughing
for the rest of that night walk
Oh, I noticed, I noticed it all
And I couldn't stop thinking
How could you be so fine
after what you just said?
Be it unintentionally
you shouldn't be alright
with your own self

I wanted to run and leave
but my feet were numb
I wanted to shout and scream
but watching you so unbothered
suppressed everything

So, instead, I walked silently
zoning in and out of reality
watching you talk and laugh
and watching me fall apart

And then, suddenly, the night walk ended
after a long time
and you went inside your house
and not long after I received your text, that said,
'I'm sorry if I hurt you. I didn't mean what I said.'

And that sorry was more heartache for me
because the moment I told you
it's inhuman to say what you just said
I was clear with my words and not hiding my anger
and you still weren't sure
you still weren't sure

So, I replied,
'Well, if you weren't so sure
you shouldn't have said sorry.'
And then you acted like I was crazy

Chaos Inside

I don't know if I'll ever get over it
I don't know if I'll ever be fine
Because every time I remember that night
it's like I'm drowning in my own mind

Because every time I remember that night
I don't understand what happens to me on the inside

I used to feel good
about us being neighbours
even though I never
said it out loud to you
And now,
I hate
that we are neighbours
because,
because, every time I see you,
every time I hear your voice
I feel like an open wound
that can never be alright

Oh, how much it hurts my head
and twists my mind
to carry this weight of your words
and to hold onto this pain
as if, as if, deep down
even I myself believe
that I deserve it
because
because it was you
who said it

Crying in my blankets late at night
I'm asking myself over and over again
Why would you say something
that terrible in front of me?
Was I so bad a friend
for you to be so cold and extreme?

Countless times
I have begged my own mind,
screamed at my own mind
to forget what you said that night
because I need it to stop,
I need it to be alright
I am exhausted
I need my sleep tonight

And then, only after
so much headache, heartache, and tears
I would doze off, barely able to breathe
then I would wake up in the morning
completely drained
and find my thoughts
playing on repeat

They say,
forgiving others for your own sake
helps you find your peace of mind

So, I tried so hard to see your side
through my eyes
even after that night
Because I needed to find
an ounce of forgiveness inside
so I could finally, finally,
feel fine inside my own mind

And in that process
Do you have any idea
how many times I have
defended you in my head?
How many times I have
gaslighted myself?
to be able to find forgiveness
for your words that night
that robbed me of my peace of mind
so I can finally, finally,
stop suffocating inside

This wasn't the first time
you used your words
without first thinking about them
in your own mind

And every single time
before that night
even if it bothered me, hurt me
I let it slide, I let it slide
thinking you were just a child
thinking that, over time, you will become better
at filtering your own words
from your own mind

Oh, how wrong I was
to take your side
Because now here I am
can't stop thinking, thinking-
Was I the reason you were so ignorant
towards your own words that night?

You went back to
talking and laughing
as if everything was right in the world
and I felt like I was over-feeling
what I felt
and that what I felt was wrong
even when all my feelings were valid,
even though
you were the one in the wrong

And sometimes I wish, I really wish,
I could hate you
and leave it at that
but I can't
I can't
because hating you would mean
hating a part of me
and there's no way
your side in me can have
that power over me

That night is burned in my memory
your words are still strangling me inside
I have lost the count of times
I have beat myself up on the inside
because I was the reason I ended up
around you that night

My mind keeps screaming
You should have known
My mind keeps draining
I should have known

Then suddenly, our good times
make their way into my thoughts
only for me to drown all over again

Oh, you would never know
you would never know
how much forgiveness costs of me
and how much not forgiving costs from me

Every time I feel like I have overcome the pain
it hits me suddenly, all over again

And that pain makes me want to
rat you out to the world
but the world doesn't deserve
your words' agony and pain

Then I think, I think
I should at least write it down
and keep it to myself
so I can at least be a step closer
to being fine again
But when I pick up my notebook and pen,
everything plays in my mind
over and over again, within seconds
all the bad, all the terrible,
all the good and all the in-between
oh, you would never know
how much I'm tortured by everything

The Other Night

I feel like a free bird
carrying the weight

You walked away, like
it was my mistake

You owed me a real apology
for a long time now
and I needed to collect it
for my own sake now

So I put us on the same road at the same time
and I heard you matching my pace from behind
as you were walking towards me tonight

But then I saw people at a distance on the street
and I thought to myself,
'You would not do it now, would you?'

And I was surprised, not surprised
when you reached beside me and said,
'We need to talk'

'Go ahead,' I said
'Let's just first cross these people standing ahead,'
you pointed with your eyes

And when we reached past the people
you asked me
'Is everything fine between us?
I don't understand what happened.
Why did you stop talking?
I think, probably, I might have done something wrong.
Was it because I did something wrong?'

At first, I felt anger
for I thought you would have
realised by now
and then I felt a relief
for I'll get to say it out loud
and let you know now
because you needed to know your fault
and I needed to be the one to tell you

So, I said,
'Remember what you said on that night walk?'
I said, 'Imagine how it would feel like
to hear what I heard you say that night
from a friend who was very close to you
at one point in time in your life.'

A second later, you said,
'I didn't realise it still bothered you,
you still had it on your mind.'
And then you asked me
if there was something else you did wrong
that I would like to tell you about tonight

And a hundred different things
floated in my mind
and all of those concluded saying
there's no point in telling,
there's no point in telling tonight

I said not a word
and you finally said your sorry
But it didn't feel like an apology
it felt like a formality

So, I barely heard you
for the next minute
as you kept talking and talking
and then I jerked out of my mind
when I heard you say
'But look at my side too'
as if it were perfectly reasonable and right

I was now so furious and outraged
I stopped walking, and I said
'What the hell do you mean your side?
Do you have any idea
how much it has hurt me?
Every time I look at you,
I remember that night
How many times thinking about
what you said that night
has kept me up at nights?'

And then, then, you said
'Okay, okay'
trying to calm me down
'I'm sorry'

My phone rang, and I answered it
distraction for a minute
had calmed me down a bit
meanwhile, you asked me
if you should leave
I waved an unclear no,
and in a minute, I cut the call
waving my hand to indicate the road

When we started walking again, you said,
'You know me too well to know
that a lot of times
I say stuff I don't mean
without even thinking.'

And all I really wanted was to ask you-
Why would you?
Why would you
say something like that
in front of me that night?
After all those years of friendship,
why would you,
why would you not care
to watch your words as you speak tonight?

But I chose not to instead,
because the truth remains
that if you really did care
you wouldn't have been so careless
so, I scoffed inside my mind instead

Now that we had walked a few metres
while you were still
talking about yourself
we had reached a place
where we used to sit for a bit
before heading back home from night walks

You asked me, 'Should we?'
waving towards the spot

I took a moment to think
and I first thought of us sitting
and talking it all out
But then, I remembered
that it would mean
taking my guard down

So, I said, 'No.'
And you said, 'Okay, okay.'
And then, we both parted ways,
I continued walking in the same direction
and you turned around to head back home

And I thought to myself,
this was the last time
this was the last time

But then, not ten feet away
I heard you say
'Wait a minute'

I stopped and turned around
and I saw you walking towards me

You said
'I understand about you. But what about those two?
Did they stop talking to me because of that night too?'

And now, I was so irritated and frustrated by you
because after everything your words did to me
you dared to ask me
'Why, my friends, who were once your friends too
stopped talking to you?
And was it because I shared with them
what your words said that night, meant that night?
Was I the reason why?'

But then I chose to keep my feelings aside
because I needed to get this over with tonight
'No,' I said, 'It's because
you stopped being their friend
so they stopped being yours
and even when they tried to approach you, call you,
you didn't reciprocate
so they saw a pattern and changed.'

And I wasn't surprised a bit when you refused
'They didn't. I can show you.'
'They did. They showed me,' I said
I said, 'Look, I'm telling you what they told me
I'm not making any of it up.'

Now, of course, you couldn't take the truth
you couldn't accept that you were in the wrong
so you said
'Okay, so you all have made this perception of me.'

And in that moment, I felt like
you were trying to turn around
the blame on me
So, in that moment, I decided,
I decided, I don't care if the truth hurts you
the truth is what you will get tonight

'No, I didn't,' I said. 'And neither did they,
we just saw a pattern and changed.'

Then you said
'Okay, fine, leave that.'
because you couldn't change my mind
so now you changed the subject instead
and said, 'I'm sorry you got hurt because of me.'
which honestly felt like winding up
so you can leave

And I barely even looked at you
because your sorry wasn't touching,
no, not even a bit
And then, suddenly, you asked me
'Do you really think I would
say something like that, that bad
intentionally?'

It grabbed my attention, and I looked at you
and I gave no answer this time
I just stood there
looking right into your eyes

And against all odds, I would have said 'NO'
so you don't have to feel bad about
what you said that night
that no matter what I had been through
you would still be alright

And for half a second there,
I was about to do that
But then, I thought about myself,
I thought about
what I had been through after that night,
I thought about
how you only cared about yourself
when I said I wasn't alright,
how barely a minute ago you asked me
to look at your side
as if it were completely, completely, right

And then, I thought about,
how wrong it would be
to not take my side this time,
about exactly how much harm I would do to myself
if I say 'no' to make sure you'll be fine

And I was well aware,
well aware, I had the choice
right in my hands
whether to break my own heart
and say it's fine
or whether to break your this time
by the truth in my mind

So, forgive me if I chose yours
because you didn't care to preserve mine that night
because you didn't care to preserve mine that night

And now, I heard your voice fumble,
I saw your eyes slowly filling with tears
as you said
'I'm sorry, I really didn't mea-'

And then, you stopped
because there was still no flicker in my eyes
not even a flinch in my disguise

Because I didn't believe a yes, nor did I believe a no
not after that night, not after tonight

And you couldn't take it
you couldn't take how rigid I was
so you stopped speaking
and left with tears in your eyes

I knew, you wanted to tell me
that you didn't mean it
But you didn't know how to
make me believe it

You couldn't take
how much my guard was up
how much I was rigid and cold
and I understood it
because I felt that too, I felt exactly
how much cold I was to you

And I know, how helpless you felt
I knew, in that moment how hurt you were
But how could I care
when your words and actions tonight
screamed at me that you didn't care?
When your apology wasn't even convincing
no, not even a bit?

So, I watched you walk away in so much pain
because I couldn't accept your apology and stop the rain
and then, suddenly, a part of me melted seeing you cry

But I wasn't going to leave my ground to comfort you
so I thought, you should at least know the truth
so I shouted behind you, and I said,
'I know you didn't mean it. I just need some time
to sink it in me.'

And I thought,
if not, say something
you would at least turn
so I stood there for a few more seconds
expecting you to recognise my effort

How foolish of me! How foolish of me!
Because you kept walking and walking
as if I were the reason you were in so much pain
as if I were to be blamed
even when it was you who had started this rain

And I felt so terrible that I cared for you
even in my pain
but you were so into yourself
that you couldn't see it again

You couldn't see
that I had just helped you out
even if just a little bit
I had helped you out with forgiving yourself
when I couldn't even muster up
my own forgiveness for you

And all of this time
I just needed one solid, heartfelt apology
not a thousand empty ones
But your pride robbed me of that too
and here, I was still caring for you

Should've Known

You broke us a million times first
only for me to do it
one last time

I should've known when,
when, everybody else knew
more about
what you were doing in your life
and people used to ask me
'What kind of a best friends are you?'
'You don't know?'

I should've known when,
when, I could see it and feel it
that even if
we went to small parties together
you would rather sit with
anybody else than with me

I should've known when,
when, your compliments
were always, always, tainted
by weird undertones

I should've known to
believe my eyes
when I noticed your promises
about our friendship
were just empty words
that could never be a line

You told me on my birthdays,
that I was special to you
only to be reminded over the year
that I didn't mean that much to you

You said,
you wanted our friendship to last
only for me to figure out
that you would leave me for the world
to be at your behest
and here I would have left the world for you
even if it was at my behest

You told me,
'You'll always be there for me'
only to find out
that you didn't care
because you never bothered to show up
when I needed you the most
to be there

You said,
No matter where you fly high in your life,
you'll always fly back to me

And that's exactly,
exactly, where the problem lies, you see
Because,
because, I don't deserve someone
who leaves
Because,
because, I deserve someone
who chooses to fly high
and go wherever they like
and yet never, never, leave my side

For my friendship is no shackle
It does not cost one for the other

And you should've known that
you should have known that

You stopped seeing through my lies
when I said, 'I'm alright'
or maybe, maybe,
you just never wanted to
I figured
because a lot was going on
with your life too

You said,
you are here for me
whenever I need you
and every time I called you,
you sounded busy

And trust me, I understood it,
I understood it better
than any of your other best friends could
but then, you yourself
accidently told me
how much time you wasted
even with your tight schedule

And I couldn't help but think, think,
you did have a minute of your month
you just, you just, never wanted to share it
with anyone, including me
you just, you just, never wanted to
check up on me

This one time
I uploaded a post on social media that said-
Some people say,
"I will be there for you
whenever you need me."
What they actually mean is,
"I will be there for you
whenever I have some extra time to waste."

And you asked me,
whether it was about you
So, I told you the truth-
it was

And then, you became
angry and defensive
and I felt bad that I hurt you,
I felt bad that I was too harsh on you

So, I took down the post
and said my sorry to you
thinking I was probably wrong about you

But now, now, when I think about it
I should've known
How, how could you've known
unless, unless, deep down you knew
that that's exactly what you were doing?

Whenever you needed to vent, I was always there
and whenever I needed to vent, I noticed, I noticed,
you wanted to escape from there

I thought it was perhaps because
you always cared more about fun
than you ever cared about emotions

And probably, I thought, it was because
I always, always, needed to vent
because my world was falling apart
while yours was perfectly intact

And even though I could see it all,
I always reminded myself
that me and my collapsing world
was too much to process
I told myself you wouldn't do it
I told myself that you probably needed more time
before you get back to me this time, this time

I should've known not to take your side,
should've known not to make myself blind
when I could see it all, as clear as a sunny day
that you didn't want to spend time with me
because you didn't care about me that much anyway

I would have let it slide, I would have let it slide
if you were a stranger who didn't know
where you hurt me
is where I am broken, is where I can never be alright

But you were there, weren't you?
when life happened
and broke me where I am broken now

You were there
and I was comforting you
keeping aside myself
that's exactly how much I cared about you

So, now, don't you tell me
I know you too well to know
that you can be stupid at times
Because I know too well-
That one doesn't hurt the people one loves
where it can hurt them the most
that one stay too careful
where the wound is sour
and that is it, that is it

And you should've known that
you should have known that

The Last Night

I need to be around you
one last time
I need answers
to stop suffering inside

I heard you every single time
you called out my name tonight
I saw every single effort
that you made tonight

Responding would be fine
or not responding would be kind
I couldn't decide, I couldn't decide

So, I choose to talk to you
when talking didn't hurt my mind
and I choose to ignore you
when I wasn't sure I was fine inside

And I knew,
I knew, you wanted to save our friendship this time
I knew, you wanted to hold on to me this time
I could see it in your eyes,
I could see it, feel it,
in the efforts you made tonight

But all I knew, was that, I deserved a better friend
than you were to me that night

All I cared, was that, I deserved a better friend
than you bothered to be that night

Walking back home
from my usual night walk
I saw a car approaching towards me
and as I walked towards it
it slowed down
and stopped right in front of me

'We are going to get some ice cream.
Would you like to come?'
my friend behind the steering wheel asked
'He is leaving tomorrow,'
he added, pointing towards another friend
sitting on the front seat, at his left
whose family was moving tomorrow

And even though I wanted to join
I was about to say 'No'
because I knew my mom wouldn't approve
for it was past eleven tonight
and also because
she was in the back seat

'Umm, okay,' I said
and I walked to the back seat door

When I opened it,
I saw her
sitting on the other side
and only then
did I realise
how much close
I have to sit to her
tonight

So, I told myself, reminded myself
again and again
Don't get warm now,
don't forget all the hurt now
Do not melt now,
please do not melt now

Let the guard be up, let the guard be up
I'm right here, I am right here

'Where are we going?' I asked
as soon as I calmed myself down
'Rajwada,'
our friend, who is leaving tomorrow, replied
And then, she said something to me
that I completely ignored tonight

And I called my little brother
who was still awake at home
to tell him
where I am, who I am with, and that
I will be a little late

Meanwhile, we reached the road
that leads to Rajwada
and now my friend, who was driving
slowed down the car a bit
and while everyone was searching
for the ice cream shops
I was lost in my own thoughts

Lost, soaking in the emptiness of the road,
lost, trying to see the dark patches and spaces
the streetlights chose to hide
lost in the outside world
or the one inside my mind

And only then
did I become aware
of where I was
when I heard the words that said
'Looks like there are no ice cream shops
nor any tea stalls open here tonight.
Let's check some other street.'

So, we turned around
tracing back the road
until another road breaks from it
the one we wanted to explore

But before we made it to that road,
we were about to pass by
the one that led to the city lights

'Should we go watch the city lights?'
our friend driving the car suggested

And all of us agreed
so he changed the road and drove
in the direction of Ghat this time
And then, a few minutes later
he stopped the car outside a shop
to get cold drinks tonight

Before getting out of the car,
she asked out loud
'What do you all want?'

And I heard the boys naming
one thing after the other
while I couldn't even figure out
how to speak

And then, I saw and heard her asking
both the boys, one by one
and then she turned towards me
and asked me
'Anything would be alright,' I said

And I knew, I knew,
it was a vague answer
I knew, I should have named properly
But I didn't know how to
so I let it be
so I let it be

She got out of the car
and walked to the shop
I lowered the window of my side
to watch the dogs on the street
walking, sleeping, standing upright
and I thought to myself tonight
'Why do I get to be the one sitting safely inside?'

In a minute or two, she was back
and I heard the car door open
and I saw her clutching the items tightly
managing to keep them in her hands

And I thought to myself,
Should I've known to pay attention?
Should I've known to help her?
out of kindness maybe, maybe

Then, I remembered, I remembered
the old version of me would've
the old version of me would have

She ducked her head in
and dumped everything
cold coffee cans, several chocolate bars
on her side of the seat

Then, she passed the cans to the boys
in the front
and one of them wanted to
change something
so she was about to go
exchange it for him
and before going
she asked, 'Do you want this too?'
showing me the cold coffee can

'Check if they have Sprite or
any other cold drink would be fine,' I said

'You want Sprite?' She asked

'Yes,' I said

In less than a minute, she was back this time
and she made herself comfortable
while the car engine started
and then she passed the exchanged item
in the front, and then she handed me
a bottle of Sprite
and a chocolate,
a chocolate I used to love
when we were best friends

I took both the things
and kept them beside me
watching out the car window
I thought to myself

'Did she remember
or was it just a random pick?'

'Well, I don't really like it now,'
I reminded myself
and forgot all about it

As the car went higher up the road
talk about which music to play
that we all knew unrolled

And I was busy looking outside
at the city lights
while jumping to Cruel Summer in my mind
and I was about to suggest it
but then I didn't
because I was way too happy inside

Finally, a song was chosen
and the Bluetooth was connected
and I heard her asking
a couple of questions about our school
that only I among us
knew the answers to

And I felt like I should answer them
I was about to
but then, suddenly, I chose not to

And then, I did something
I know I shouldn't have-
I answered the same question
when someone else asked

Not long after, we found a good spot
where the mountain curve was not too close
and the road was wide enough to park

I picked up my cold drink
while everyone picked up their cans
and we all entered
the pleasant cold outside

And I saw her hop onto
the roadside barrier first
and I made sure I hopped on and sat
the farthest from her

While the boys were still standing
behind the barrier, in the distance I had
placed between us
the cans and the bottle
were opened and consumed

And the city lights were
covered by a mist
or probably by the drizzles in the city
whatever it may be
it made the city lights
even more beautiful to see

The boys placed their empty cans
on the barrier in front of them
after the cold coffee was consumed
and one of the cans stumbled and went down
with the breeze

Talk about
'Should've known not to keep it there.'
floated around
and I was about to pick the other one up
when I saw one of the boys push it down

'You shouldn't have done that,'
the other guy exclaimed
And then, she and I,
we both were telling him
why not to do it again
saying the same things
in different words,
saying the same words
in different sentences

And when I noticed it,
I wondered if she did
because I don't know
if she was looking at me
because I know I wasn't
no, not even a bit

A few minutes later, the boys hopped on too
talk about colleges, manifestation
and several other things floated too

Now, the city lights had become
brighter than before
maybe the mist had subsided a bit
or maybe because the drizzle had stopped in the city

Would be a good movie scene I thought to myself
and I wished we could stay a little longer
but we had to head back home

So, now, I got into the car first
and when she opened the door next
I saw a few chocolates covering her seat
and I pulled them in the middle
so she could get in

And I was surprised by myself
because I thought, after that night
I had no kindness in me for her tonight

And that the kindest thing I would do for her
is to not talk, is to not engage
so that I don't blast onto her
Was it reasonable or not?
was not the question here

And when we reached home,
one of the boys said,
'Let's make it a movie night,
what do you say?'

'Which movie?' I heard myself say
and only then did it occur to me
that I probably shouldn't have
that I probably shouldn't join
because most of our movie nights
used to happen in the same house
and probably as will of tonight

'An old one,' he said
and meeting up
in ten minutes was decided

'I will go and change,' I said
while everyone was still standing there
and as I walked towards my home
and away from everyone
I turned around and asked the boys,
'Where are we going to watch it?'
because I needed to confirm it

'At her house,' a boy said
pointing towards her

'Okay,' I said

At home, as I freshened up
and changed into comfy clothes
I kept wondering to myself
Should I back out somehow? Should I say no?

And then, I thought to myself,
'No, this would be the last time, the last night
we all spend time together
and I don't want to back out of that
and besides, I need to see
that, after all, she is a human
to let her mistake be.'

So, standing outside her house,
I called onto one of the guy's names first
then I knocked, and she opened the door

And barely even looking at her
I walked in the door and entered the hall
where the boys and her mom were sitting, talking
and I walked straight to the farthest divan
I always used to sit on
and she sat next to her mother

Memories of the school days
were breathing in the room again
and unlike other times, this time
even for just a little bit
I joined in the conversation tonight

Laughter making room
every ten seconds
I watched your mother laugh too
from the bottom of her heart

And I remembered something
I had refused myself to think of

I remembered exactly how many times
I had ignored your parents in their faces
because they would ask me of you
and I couldn't tell them the truth

Because I kept thinking to myself
What if I blabber out the truth
even more bitterly than it already is?
What if I give them a hard time?
Because I wasn't sure they were aware
that you had given me plenty after that night

Feeling terrible for ignoring your parents
for having to ignore your parents
I snuck into the conversation again
and I noticed
the topic was changed

That the topic had now landed onto
the memories of previous movie nights

And as everyone was
talking and laughing tonight
I saw the pictures clearly in my mind
of all the past times

And I saw how much I was in the background
and not exactly a part of the memories
most of the time, that most of the times
even if I was present in the room
my presence was only in the nods and smiles

Suddenly, the room fell silent
but my mind did not

My mind
thought about the times
I saw you
in small gatherings twice
before this last night,
before tonight

And as I watched you,
from a distance
then and now
I wondered and wondered
'What made you so special
for me to get so badly hurt now?'

'Let's go, watch a movie,'
someone reminded again

We all got up and walked to your room
and my thoughts walked with me too,
and I remembered this one time
when my parents and my little brother
were going on a family vacation
and I was not
your mom said to me
that I can sleep in your room at nights
that you were in college
so your room wasn't occupied
to which I kindly refused

And as I entered your room,
on the last night
it felt so different tonight
but not as much as I did
this version of me
who loved hanging out in your room
seemed so far out of reach

'Let's play a game,' she said
when we all sat down in her room

'No, we are not in the mood,'
one of the guys, and I said

'Come on, just two rounds,'
she and the other guy insisted

And then, suddenly, out of nowhere,
I saw myself giving up my ground
because I was too used to doing it
when I thought we were best friends for life
and tonight it had finally, finally,
caught up to me now

So, I downloaded the game on my phone
only to find out
that I have to ask her for some code
so I had to talk to her
and when I did, I noticed, I noticed
in how much of a better way
you were answering my questions
when I was barely even
communicating them

'This is all I can muster up,'
I heard myself say
'Okay okay,' I comforted myself

The game was not exactly new to me
for it was no different than the usual ones
except for the visuals, of course

In the game,
a bunch of minions were running around
jumping and ducking
in order to survive and win the game
all minions computerised except for us

The game started
and a few seconds into it
I lost and failed
for I couldn't get the hang of it
for I really didn't want to

And I was still watching
all the minions running
trying to figure out
where my friend's minions are

And then, I heard you
call my name out loud tonight
and I heard what you said
but I didn't know how to acknowledge that
I wasn't sure if I wanted to acknowledge that

So, leave it be, I thought instead
let it be, I told myself

What if I'm too blinded by your faults
to actually see mine?
I thought to myself
What if I'm rolling in self-pity
which is why
I can't understand your side?

But now, I thought again
now, that I have understood mine
I am sorry
but I can't have you
anywhere near me
for the rest of my life
not after that night
not after that night

And no good, no good
changes the fact that
tonight is the last night

For the second game
I lasted a few more seconds
than the previous one

And fortunately
a few minutes later now
the game time was over
and we decided to watch
Jab We Met

So, the lights were switched off
and she played it on her laptop
how interesting, I thought

And while watching the movie too,
I sat the farthest from you
because now I was afraid
I would
melt around you

The movie was fun,
it made us all giggle and laugh
and halfway through the movie
she brought snacks

She passed it towards me too,
and I refused
said I had my retainers on
said I can't remove them now

Besides, I thought it was bad enough
that I wasn't treating her right
bad enough
I couldn't leave my subtle attitude
out the door
when I entered her house tonight
bad enough
I thought accepting water was fine
so now I don't think I should
accept her hospitality
and eat the snacks tonight

But watching you
make efforts tonight
watching you
so patiently try
I wonder, I wonder,
maybe from now on
you will
filter your words right
I wonder
if I should
give you a chance tonight

Because they say
friendships can become new
sometimes, all you have to do
is give it a chance

But then, another part of me
decides and declares-
I'm not going to put myself to test
for both of you to ace or scar

Soon, the break was over
and the movie was continued

Soon, we reached the climax
to see Geet forgiving Anshuman
despite him not accepting her at first
despite all she had been through

And I realised, I realised, that the movie
wasn't just pointing towards the fact that
'The wrong person will never, never,
think you are enough.'
but it was also pointing towards
how Geet saw Anshuman
wearing blindfolds of love

And I thought to myself,
I did the same with you
I did the same with you

I saw you
wearing these blindfolds of
love of friendship
all of this time
which is why
it was so hard for me
to let go of that night

But now,
that they have fallen off
the weight has fallen off too

And now, finally, finally,
I feel light inside

Feels like
forgiveness has sparked inside
towards you, towards me
towards the both of us tonight

Now, the movie night ended
while the morning was still dark
and we all got up
to go back to our homes
with sleep in our eyes

She opened her umbrella
to drop me first
when we all were standing
at her front door
as it was raining outside

And I refused
said I was fine,
said it wasn't pouring
that much anyway outside

And I went into my house
feeling somewhat
close to being fine

I needed to see
you are, after all, a human
so that forgiveness
might do its trick
and take my pain away

And it did work for me, it did work for me
because I have found forgiveness for you,
for your words that night
as I have spent the last night
in the same room as you yesterday night

And now, I can finally, finally,
breathe in my own mind

And now, I think I can, I can,
let this all go, and
let myself be fine
because I deserve to be alright
I deserve to be fine

The next day
I called my two best friends
to meet me
to tell them
all about the last night
to recite them
this tale of forgiveness
that I have found inside

'We are happy for you'
they said to me
'I am happy for me too'
I told them

And I promised to myself
I would never, never, put me
through any of this again

Not with her
not with anybody else
I promised I would be better
for myself

And for a day there, I thought
I had overcome the pain
For a day there, I thought
I was fine again

Only to wake up to realise
two days after the last night
that that the forgiveness was fake

Because every time I remember that night
it's back to feeling terrible again
Because every time I think of you
I end up in so much pain

And no matter how much I say,
you are the cause of this pain
I am well aware
I am the reason it has stayed

Because sometimes,
I forget how to forgive you, for that night,
even for my own sake

Was It Me?

Was I too busy
reading in between the lines
when I should have
without even blinking, thinking,
focused on the words instead?

I always thought,
thought it was my
wavering confidence
that made me doubt
my own abilities
in front of you,
when I was with you

But now, as I have
grown over time
I am not sure that's the reason why
because if it were true, I would have,
I would have, felt the same
with everyone else too,
which I didn't
and that is indeed the truth

And of course, of course,
I have my moments
but never, never,
like the ones I had
when I was with you

When you first started pulling yourself away
I remember my life was full of pain

And I kept telling myself
that you just need more time to process
because my collapsing world
was too much to take in
and my energies were too draining

I kept telling myself
that you wouldn't do it intentionally
because I am your best friend
and you just need more time
on your end

So, now, I know, I know,
It was me, it was me,
who wore myself the blindfold

So, now, I know, I know,
It is me, it is me,
who is to be blamed for
playing a huge part in my own pain

You would never know, you would never know,
how much it hurts to know
that my side was always, always, tainted
by yours, all of this time
that's exactly how much importance
I gave you in my life

You would never know,
how much it pains to know
that I always cared about your her
more than I ever cared about
my her, all of this time
that's exactly how much I put you first
in my life

You would never know,
how much it aches to know
that it was me, it was me,
who put you first, all of this time
that it was me, it was me,
who wronged me
before you ever did
from the beginning of our time

Tonight, I couldn't help but ask myself
Was it me?

Was it me who doomed our friendship?
Was it me who tossed it away?
Was it me who ruined it for you and me
before that night?
Am I the one who is to be blamed?

And sometimes, when I think about that night,
I still end up asking myself

Was it me who made you so okay
to be so cruel towards me?
Was it me
who never set proper boundaries?
Was it me? Was it me?

My mind is playing a hundred
different conversations,
showing me a hundred
different memories

Giving me a hundred
different suggestions,
while also showing me
a hundred different ways
I could've handled it

Saying I am the reason why
our friendship is non-existent today

But how can it be?
I ask myself,
when a friendship takes two people to be

Tonight

I walk, and walk, and walk,
unintentionally tracing
that night's and the other night's paths
My mind talks, and talks, and talks,
about nothing and then everything non-stop

I was a nest for you to come home
or was I an anchor holding you to the shore?
I would never know
I would never know

You started to keep your life a secret from me,
was it because I wasn't in good energies
or because you didn't think it's good to share
your life's information
with just anyone, including me?
I would never know
I would never know

You changed and stopped caring first,
was it because I was all dark blue
or was it because your world was bright new?
I would never know
I would never know

I would never know
who and what I was for you
because if you really did care
as you said so yourself
I would have always, always, said
I know, I know

Eighth grade was the first time
I saw how lonely you felt in your life
I saw how much you wished
you had siblings
to keep you company at times

So, I decided to fill that space in your life,
to keep you company
so you don't have to feel lonely
all the time
but in our friendship of years
even when you were there
I was the one who felt lonely
almost all the time

And no,
I still don't really regret
letting you in
but sometimes
I get so tired of thinking, and thinking,
about the first time
I let you in,
about the first reason why
I let you in

You could've been considerate and kind
when I was going through a hard time
but you choose to be
distant and ignorant
even when you had time

I thought friends can see
right through you
but you believed my lies,
you believed the show I put on
of being strong and fine

So, now, do tell me
How can I remember the good times?
when you were practically
ignoring me at my worst

How can I say
you were a good friend of mine?
because when I needed
your presence the most
I saw you
trying your best
to hide

You left for college that year
only to leave from my life forever

And here, I waited for you
to come back to me
because, because, that's what
best friends do I thought, I thought

And you did come back for vacations
whenever you could
but you refused to come back into my life
because your life was now shiny
and mine, mine, was anything
but bright

So, eventually, I stopped waiting
and I dropped the thread
holding our friendship together
and I took a couple of steps back, thinking,
thinking, now I would watch you
watch me walk away
and that would jerk you awake
but when I reached far, far, away
only then did I saw
that you'd dropped it first
and that you had left
long back in the past

We were just kids
trying to figure out
where we fit into this world
when you put yourself in authority
in our group of friends, when we were young

And we let you
because you said, you behaved, you acted
like you knew better than any of us
and you went along with it
for many, many, years

But now, I can see, the distance has shown me
that you were just trying to figure things out
for yourself too
except you had more help
than any of us did, and that's true

It showed me
exactly how much you have
misused the power that we gave you
how much you confused us
and then left us to ourselves

Oh, you have no idea
how much your 'I know it all' attitude
has cost me from myself

Tracing the same path we walked the other night
I am full of anger, full of rage tonight

You want me to understand your side
after what you said in front of me that night?

But do you even know how many times
what you said has cost me my peace of mind?

Do you even realise how many times I have
struggled to breathe in my own mind?

How many times I have
downed inside
before I had to learn to save myself
and be alright?

Do you? Do you?

Then how could you,
why would you,
ask me to look at your side
when you didn't even bother to think of
what I might have faced after that night?
Because no, I owe you no apology
for you being stupid that night

I saw you twice the other night
and the second time I saw you
you were so fine
when barely an hour ago
we had parted ways for real this time

And I hated to see you alright
when your words and you, once again
had messed up so much with my mind

I hated to see you laugh
because even if I hated how much
self-centred you were tonight
I was still blaming myself
in the back of my mind
for making you cry

And now, I hate myself
for caring about you
all of this time
But I am also glad
I got to see you twice tonight
because seeing you fine
has crushed the part of me
that cared for you
all of this time

I told you to be careful
instead, you kept on hurting me
I said, 'Watch what you speak'
but you refused to listen to me

And you say
'I don't mean it'
How am I supposed to
believe it?

And even after every thing
here I was, here I was,
drowning in the pain
of not being a good friend

Here I was
asking myself
Was it me?
over and over again

Tonight, I'm watching us part ways again
watching the other night play in front of me again

And tonight, I am seeing everything differently
I'm seeing, how after all your empty apologies
you turned around
to blame me, tame me
just when I'd thought
you can stoop no lower, you did, you did

And yet, while trying to stand my ground
I was also trying my best not to hurt you
because the truth was hurtful enough

So, now, all I want to say
to you and your doubt
about me making a perception of you, is-
Believe what you may
I no longer care anyway

All of this time,
I didn't allow myself to write
all the chaos I faced inside

Because I knew, I knew,
when I write it all down
I would, I would, want to
share it with the world tonight

And I kept thinking to myself,
that if I let it all out
that if I talk about my emotions out loud

I thought it would rob you
of your chance to be a better person
than you were that night
that I could, would, be the reason
you might find it difficult
to find forgiveness inside

So, all of this time
I pushed it too hard,
locked it away
in my own thoughts

But now, that I have
let it all out
now, that my rage has calmed down,
my mind has spoken everything that it wants to

Now, that I have stopped spirailling inside,
stopped struggling to get my words right

Now, that the rain has become a drizzle,
I can see clearly now
because now, everything's laid in front of my eyes
as clear as a cloudy blue sky

I can see that
that the reason why you looked at your words
as merely words
is because imagining the pain that I went through
is beyond your imagination
because you couldn't understand
the depths of my emotions

So, now, I am going to
stop taking it personally
for my own sake now

And I know
it's a long road
before I would mean it
that tonight
even if I have written down
all of my pain
I might go back to it
tomorrow again

Because there are times
I forgive you
when I can't remember that night
and there are also times when
even the thought of forgiveness
drowns me in my own mind

And I know it's a long road
so I have started walking tonight
hoping I would make it one day
one step at a time

And I really, really, wish
you hadn't put me
in so much pain
I really, really, wish
I could change that night
for myself again

But I can't
I can't

So, I would rather make this
into something
I would be less tortured by
than care about your side

So, I would rather make sure
I won't have to
guard the door
Because now I know for sure
you will not visit anymore

A part of me wanted to label it as your fault
and leave it at that tonight

Because I couldn't gulp down the truth
that there was a time
when we were best friends
and then there is tonight, we are not

And it was easier for me to blame you
for every wrong thing
before that night too
because my not writing had clouded
my own judgment, that's true

But then, one day,
I found our scraps of conversations
and after weeks, I read it tonight

And I saw the truth that said
you are not the only one
who is to be blamed
for dooming our friendship
before that night

I saw that
when I said-
'I don't see any efforts from your side'
you made them
and I didn't even appreciate them

For your definition of friendship and mine
could never be a line
Because you had fun in your mind
and I had too many deep conversations inside

So, tonight, I now know
and no matter
how hard it might be
for me to admit it
I will, I will

So, tonight, I now know-
That it wasn't just you or me
who failed our friendship
before that night
It was the both of us
It was the both of us

And maybe this is where it all went wrong
on my side in our friendship-
me tainting my side with yours all the time
me putting your side above mine
which is why I always felt unseen from you
when, in real, I was the one not seeing myself

But now that I have written it all out,
I can see both sides of our coin

And I guess this is where it all went wrong
in our friendship on both of our sides-
There shouldn't have been a coin,
there shouldn't have been a side

No, not in a friendship, no
and with that being said
I am not saying I was wrong to feel
what I felt on my end before that night,
or that I don't trust what I felt anymore
because I respect my feelings
and I'll leave it at that tonight

I don't believe
in returning the same hurt
back where it came from
and this might seem exactly that to you

But what does it matter now?
For that night was when you truly lost me
and this book is where I know
I will truly lose you

So, I'll do this for myself
I'll write down everything
and share
so I can be fine again

Because this I know tonight-
That whatever be the reason
for you saying whatever you said
in front of me that night
I now know, clearly in my mind
that no one deserves it
that I didn't deserve it

Letters

Unread, Unsent, Unsaid words
that sometimes soothe me
sometimes haunt me
at nights

Dear you in my head,

I fought with you on texts
oh-so-many times
not to hurt you
but to tell you
what wrong I felt was coming
from your side to mine
and to know for sure if the errors
were only on my side

But all you heard
was blaming
All you could see
was shaming

So, I still don't know
if I am in the wrong or right
because your side in me
is still clouding my judgement tonight

But I know this alright
that I wasn't the only one
who felt all of this
every night

Dear you after that night,

I know there were good times
but I can't remember them

I know there was happiness floating around
but all I end up remembering is pain

Not because I hate you that much
which I don't
But because
every time I want to remember the good times,
I have to first go through
unveiling that night
because that night is cloaking everything good
there ever was before that night
before that night

And I wish I could change that for you
but I can't

And I wish I could change that for me
which I know I can, but I still can't

Dear you before that night,

I never was loud around people
about how much
our friendship meant to me
and how much I loved you
And I knew that was my problem,
so I, I made sure, I showed it to you
in the small things I did for you

And I still remember all of those times
when you introduced me
as your best friend in front of people
and all I could do was smile

I guess that's what doomed our friendship, don't you?
my inability to make you feel seen and heard in public
and yours to make me when we were not in public

Perhaps we might have learned it over time,
perhaps we might have become better over time
But we both couldn't make ourselves to make an effort
so I guess it's better now
than later in life

Dear me,

I am so, so, sorry honey
I gave her more importance than you
all of this time

I am so, so, sorry honey
I should have seen you and your side
before anyone else's

If I could walk back in the past and change it,
I want you to know that I would, I would
And going forward in the future
I will choose you before anyone else
I will, I will

Dear Sister,

I am so, so, sorry I was off chasing someone
who didn't care about us
when I should've known
not to do that
when I should have known
that you are the one
I should have been with
I should have cherished the most

And now that I know
I will always, always,
treasure you in my heart
the most

Dear all of you,

For so long, I kept pushing this story aside
For so long, I didn't do the one thing
that I knew would make me fine

Because telling the truth of my side
still feels like
blaming you, shaming you
Because this is how I know
you will perceive it tonight

So, no, this isn't about making you pay
this is about me finding my own way
Because I know no other way to heal
than to freeze it in time
so others can read

And no, this isn't a mean book
intended to exploit your flaws
But it is my truth
that I could no longer hide from

And yes, I know you won't believe me now
when I say the truth out loud tonight-
That it hurts way too much to tell this tale
But it hurts more to keep it locked away in a cage

Dear Reader
I cannot have ended this book
without writing to you

Writing to say
THANK YOU FOR READING SIDES

Writing to say
that, if you have ever experienced
what I have
to which I hope the answer is no
but just in case it's a yes
just in case it's something that we share

I want you to know that
I am well aware of what they say
about letting things go
that they say-
'Letting go is a necessary part of moving on'

So, I want you to know
that I don't think it is
that I think letting go is the wrong way to go
that I think what we need to do is
make peace with it

And when I say peace,
I do not mean in a way
that invalidates everything
When I say peace
I mean it in a way
that holds space for everything

Creating space by
writing, talking, painting about it
by any creative means
that we need to, want to choose
to express about it

To sit with it
and validate it to its very core
to love it to its very core
so your you that felt the pain doesn't feel
unloved anymore

Because however bad
this experience might be
the thoughts of letting go and my attempts
to get rid off of a part of me
created a much bigger chaos inside,
trust me

And dear reader
I might be wrong
I might just be writing to you
from the part in me
that just refuses to let it all go

Because honestly
making peace with it
doesn't take the pain away

But if I am being honest with you
I will also say
letting it be,
letting it creatively exist inside me
has calmed down all the chaos
I once felt inside me